List Building

Pro Blogger and YouTuber Shares his Secrets

Brendan Mace

Table of Contents

FREE BONUS: List Building Video Series

Click Here to Get Your FREE Bonus

Introduction

"Being broke is a choice. You're just lazy!" Growing up in a working class family, that's the attitude. I get the ambition of it, but who would actually choose to have no money? I used to wear the same smelly uniform, five days a week. I would have changed clothes, but my employer, let's call him "Dave," declined to provide more than one company T-shirt -- I declined to wash it every day. Despite being a 'Thousandaire,' Dave would shudder at the idea of wasting money on a worker. My boss was a dick. He was the kind of guy that gave out the minimum, and expected the maximum in return. You already know my story -- don't you? Every self-made marketer's situation is different, but the pattern is usually the same.

My name is Brendan Mace. I grew up in a working class family that always had food on the table, but perpetually served the rich. It was a life that was comfortable -- not the one I wanted. One day I stumbled on a marketing blueprint that would change the course of my life. I don't even remember what this product was called, just that it promised boatloads of money and fancy cars for about the price of a StarBucks latte. I was hooked. I read every word of that twenty page Ebook. I thought I had found the Holy Grail of Marketing. This was exactly what I needed to stick my middle finger up at the 9-5, I would say to myself. Unfortunately, life doesn't always work out the way you want it too. I can tell you now that I wish what this blueprint promised were true. Like everyone reading this, I wanted the big home, the frequent vacations and the fancy Lamborghini in the driveway. I wanted all of these things, most of all, as quickly as I could dream them up.

The next few years were rough. I would have settled for a Rolls Royce, but my results were staggering. As in, I didn't have any. I tried everything in the book: Ebay, SEO, websites and even scrapping for money on Fiverr.com (a website that pays $5 per task). The life lessons I endured during this intensely challenging time would prove invaluable.

What you will learn in this book is the real road map that I've used to make a full time income online. There's no misleading information, or outdated methods that will waste your time. Take action on the advice in these chapters, and you won't have to work a "job" again in your life. You will learn the biggest lesson of them all: you don't find the Holy Grail of Marketing -- you create it.

Back to my story…

"WHAT THE #@C#^@ HAPPENED?" screamed my boss at a barely unnoticed volume. It was the middle of the lunch rush at Dave's Diner, and I was the only server in the restaurant. My boss angrily pointed at a grumpy old lady with makeup that looked as if she was auditioning for the local circus community. I felt a lump in my throat. When moments like this happen, there's really nothing you can do. I rang in the wrong order, and the lady was pissed. If I talked back to my boss, I would likely be fired. This job was the only thing that paid the bills. Even though I hated it, the money was better than any of my other options at the time. I had fantasized about quitting for years, but the risk of unemployment is scary. So I stayed, and the weeks passed. While daydreaming about a better life, I would picture myself on a beach with a laptop. I had already been marketing for a few years, so my subconscious knew the easiest way out. I had a choice:

continue struggling at a job I hate, or learn how to make money online. So I sat down, and I ran through my options.

I kept hearing people talking about list building. There's this annoying little cliché that you can't help but notice: "the money is in the list." I had always avoided email marketing, because the idea to me seemed to be too complicated. Why not just set up a website, and get free traffic from Google? That would be easy. All you have to do is write up some content, and let the search engines bring in the visitors. The problem was, I had already tried that. With no exaggerations, I have created more than fifty different websites. Then I realized what my business was missing. I didn't control my traffic. My entire business was dependent on Google's whimsy.

And that's when I had my big "AHA" moment. Successful marketers don't wait for business to come to them. They control the money they make, and actively create a system to get it. I needed to control my traffic. The easiest way to control traffic is to go to the traffic store and buy it. This may seem scary to you, it sure as hell was for me. But when you buy traffic, you usually get higher quality visitors, and you can get predictable results. The solution became simple: I need to make $2 for every $1 I spend. As long as I make more money than I spend, I can buy as much traffic as I want.

Within two weeks of this epiphany, I quit my job for good. Now I make over $10,000 every month, and travel the world for fun. The rest of this book shares the results and methods from my journey, and encourages you to accomplish your dreams.

Chapter 1 – The Simple Two Step Formula

A lot of people talk about how to make money with lists, but not many people actually go into any detail.

Today I'm going to take you behind the scenes of my $5,000 a month business that takes me around 20 minutes per day to maintain.

On top of that, I'm going to share my personal 110+ email autoresponder sequence with you so you can learn how to do the same.

At the end of this tutorial you will have learned how to create a list building funnel that brings in new profit and leads every single day.

What You Will Learn

- My 2 step list building formula
- How to create your own list building business
- How to build an auto responder sales funnel
- How to buy traffic & make instant money
- How to build & maintain a relationship with your list automatically

My Experience:

My name is Brendan Mace, I run BrendanMace.com and the Brendan Mace YouTube Channel and this is the story of how I work less than four hours per week, but still managed to build 40K+ leads in *less than a year* on a shoe string budget.

Having over 40,000 email subscribers at your fingertips means daily affiliate commissions and free traffic anywhere you want.

More importantly though, it's easy, cheaper than you think and only takes about 20 mins per day to maintain.

By working faithfully eight hours a day you may eventually get to be boss and work twelve hours a day.

Imagine waking up on **YOUR** terms. No early commute in traffic. Waiting in your car, behind a line of exhaust-filled vehicles. Desperately needing a shot of espresso to keep yourself awake just long enough to endure **8** full hours of your employer's BS.

That's a scary story, that unfortunately, relates to wayyyyy too many of us. Your life can be different. Mine is. I escaped. Let me tell ya how…

==> **PASSIVE INCOME** <==

The secret sauce to building virtual assets with RESIDUAL income is creating a repeatable business model.

"Why hustle for hours to make the same income, when you can almost as easily create something with recurring profits? Once they're up and running, it can rake in profits FOREVER.

Just set it and forget it!"
– Ron Popeil, Founder of RONCO – Over $1 billion in revenue

Set what??

…What the F#$K is *"it?"*

In affiliate marketing terms, "it" could be a wide variety of things. Some of which include: niche sites, Facebook Pages, T-shirt campaigns, YouTube channels, Kindle books, arbitrage and so on…

In this post, we're building a ***virtual sales funnel***.

Once set up, this funnel will:

  • Provide value
  • Collect leads
  • Generate sales

And the best part, building an email list is creating a virtual property that can net you MUCH MORE than the J-O-B, for a LOT less work.

"[Luke] I can't believe it.
[Yoda] That is why you fail."

—Star Wars

Ok okay… Last quote, I promise. How could I resist Star Wars?

Anywho, this blog post is not your typical, press these buttons and watch as your bank account explodes with affiliate commissions.

NOPE… It ain't that easy.

That being said, if you break down this formula into it's separate parts, it won't be that hard either.

My "Rocket Science" Two-Step Formula:

  • Step 1: Build a List
  • Step 2: Promote Stuff

You don't need to create your own product. And you don't need to worry about specific details, like when to send and how many affiliate products to promote, etc.

Sure, there are guidelines to follow. But as long as you're building a list and notifying them about "cool stuff" as it comes out, you will make money with this...

Chapter 2 – The Ethical Bribe

The reality is that you're not going to have subscriber numbers like these overnight:

I knew that building a list was going to be a gradual process. What I didn't realize is that you can actually make a lot of money while you build your list. But more on that later…

We're starting at the beginning, which means **building your landing page.**

For those of us unfamiliar to the term "landing page" it literally just means a page on your site that is designed to collect email subscribers.

The way it works is simple, your task is to perform an ethical bribe.

An "ethical bribe" in marketing, is a promise of value in exchange for an email address.

- You get subscribers
- They get value

What Can You Give Away Of Value?

Chances are, especially if you're an active reader of Matt's blog, that you have internet marketing knowledge that would benefit other people.

Your freebie could be:

- a video
- an ebook
- a blog post

Just something that adds value. A lot of people get freaked out about this step. *That's unnecessary.* You don't need to giveaway a secret marketing method that only you know about.

As long as some people don't know (or have) your freebie and you're helping them reach their goals, your freebie is just fine.

Don't Want To Create Your Own Freebie?

You don't even have to… If you're determined to avoid this step, you can STILL be successful. Goes to show that there are MANY ways to make income with sales funnels.

One option is to embed an informative YouTube video on your blog and then send them to your blog for your freebie. You could even add your own affiliate links into your blog post and collect a little extra **BONUS** income from this strategy.

Another valid work-around is to purchase PLR (private label rights) products. What this means, is that someone took the time to create an entire product or freebie and then is selling the rights to brand this product as your own.

The real advantage of option 2 is that you get to position yourself as an authority. By slapping your name on a high quality PLR product, you appear like an expert in your field.

Even though you literally spent only a few minutes to add your name and branding to the packaging.

Here's a PLR catalog with a lot of top notch stuff: HQ Biz in a Box

Take a look at a couple examples…

Ex. 1 –List Building PLR Package

Ex. 2 – SEO Made Easy PLR Package

Pretty cool stuff, huh?

These PLR packages are completely DONE-FOR-YOU with sales pages, squeeze pages, free reports and follow up emails.

The point is, you have options:

- Create your own freebie
- Steal someone else's (i.e. YouTube Video)
- Buy PLR and rebrand it

I have personally used all three options in separate funnels and they all get the job done. Pick you own plan of attack and let's move on to the bribing!!

Bribing Cold Traffic With Your Awesome Freebie?

Get your freebie and let's create a landing page that makes it desirable.

My freebie is a video series that I created on my Two Step Formula. Sound familiar? It's the exact strategy that I'm giving away in this post. You can see my video series here.

Two Step Formula:

- Step 1: Build List
- Step 2: Promote

My Freebie: Video Series on "Make Money Online"

Now we need to take this (or your) freebie and design a page that promises it in exchange for email addresses.

In marketing, this is called a squeeze page.

Here's the one I created for this freebie:

You'll notice a few things about this squeeze page, but let's break it down.

Chapter 3 – How to Get a 56% Conversion Rate

First thing…

My landing page is really simple. It has a headline, an image, some share buttons, and an opt-in box.

This simplicity is intentional. Simple squeeze pages convert way better. The more you add to squeeze pages, the lower they convert.

Most visitors from cold traffic have an attention span of 5 seconds or less. They're like goldfish. They visit your page, make a snap judgement and then move on.

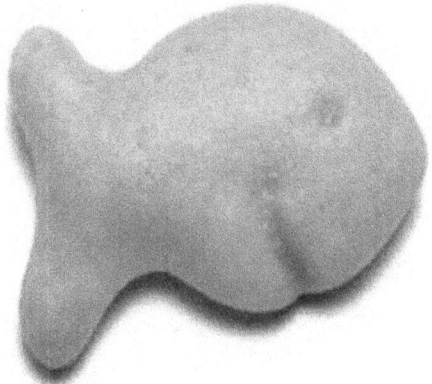

Hey, I'm not being judgemental. I'm a **goldfish** visitor, too. Other than Facebook, YouTube and a few others, I'll only invest a few seconds on your page before I decide whether to stay.

You need to grab visitor's attention and clearly give your proposition of value, but it all needs to be done in a matter of a few seconds. Tough task.

Less is more, but the less is still important. It needs to have curiosity.

Second thing…

A good squeeze page creates optimistic curiosity. It leaves a little to the imagination. Think of the squeeze page as the lingerie to the… well, you know…

In this squeeze page, I tell visitors about a mysterious **"Two-Step Formula"** that leads to near instant riches.

What 2-Step formula? Is it going to cost me anything?

… I don't tell them anything. That is, I'm not telling until they give me their email address.

Get it?

Curiosity is a h*** of a drug. It gets people in. They have to know, it's just human nature.

So to here's what you need for a successful squeeze page:

- Simple (clear to visitors within seconds)
- Proposition of value (you will make money with this)
- Curiosity (secret ingredient that significantly boosts opt-ins)

Overall, that squeeze page is averaging a **58.62%** Opt-in rate. The industry avg is around 30-40%... I'm not saying this to brag (well maybe just a little), but the main take away is that a good squeeze page is simple... BUT makes sure that every word counts.

How to Create A Winning Headline

The headline is the most important element on your squeeze page. It will make and break your conversion rate and in general, should be tested and tweaked many times.

But as a starting point, let's throw one together real quick.

When I was first learning how to create these, I was fortunate enough to stumble across an article from Eben Pagan that revealed a number of powerful headline formulas.

I'm going to share two of them with you now.

Headline Formula #1: The Quick n' Easy

This one combines three elements into a single headline and it works like this.

How to [insert benefit here] in [a short amount of time] with [very little work]

Example: How to Easily Get 150+ Email Subscribers in the Next 24 Hours

You'll notice that the example headline doesn't exactly match the order of the template. But that's really beside the point.

The key here is that your headline promises an exceptionally good result, in a quick amount of time with very little work.

It doesn't matter how you order it, as long as it includes all three elements.

Headline Formula #2: Your Problem, my Fix

This one's pretty simple. Explain what's going wrong and then hint at a solution.

Why [this typical method] is [not working]... and what to do...

Example: Why list building no longer works like it used to... and what to do about it

This one is meant to position yourself as the person with THE solution.

Everyone else is doing the same old thing and it's no longer working. Let me show you what does.

This headline can be really powerful and it's obvious why it works so well. Most subscribers are looking for that one secret or tool that will take them over the edge and finally make money online.

You're telling them that you have the answer.

Perfect!! We've covered headlines. Thanks Pagan.

Designing Your Squeeze Page

I'm going to be 100% transparent here… I've never designed a squeeze page from scratch, ever. Notta single one. Nada. Zilch.

And honestly, unless you are exceptionally skilled at graphic design and/or do-it-yourself projects, then you're way better off doing it the easy way.

Outsource it or get an awesome **head start**

My shortcut to creating *outrageously* high converting landing pages is WP Profit Builder.

It's a tool that does 95% of the design process for you. The ONLY thing you need to do is adjust the text. That's it.

The way Profit Builder works is simple. It's a WordPress Plugin that loads dozens of squeeze templates into your blog.

These templates are already top notch quality pages. So pretty much, everything is done-for-you.

Here are some examples:

Ex. 1 – High Converter

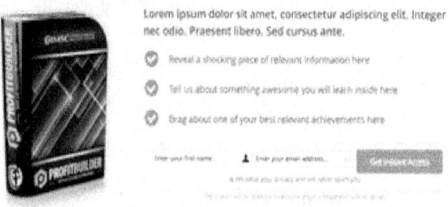

Ex. 2 – Bloom

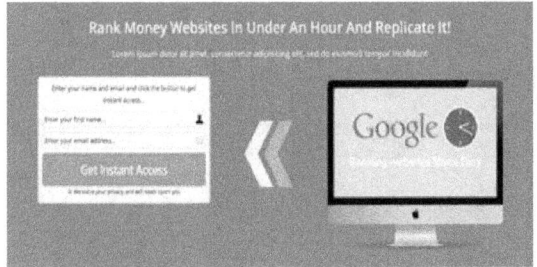

Ex. 3 – Exotic

Last template look familiar to you?

It should! It's the same template I used to create my current squeeze page as shown above.

You'll notice that I did very little to change the template. Just clicked a couple buttons, uploaded a replacement photo and edited the text. All in – it took me about 5-6 minutes of work.

… And my current squeeze page regularly gets over 55% opt-in rates. As a point of reference, the industry average is around 30%.

Not too shabby for a few minutes of my time.

The good news is that you can do this, too. It may take you a bit longer than 5 minutes. But I'd bet within half an hour you could create a real good looking page.

You could also use LeadPages or something like OptimizePress if you already have them to create something similar.

Chapter 4 – The Instant Offer

In chapter 4, we swing on to step #2… Promote stuff!!

There's a real sweet spot here. We don't want to ONLY send promotions – that'll burn our list into bits.

We need to build at least some kind of good-will with our subscribers.

On the flip side, we can't only focus on providing value and neglect promotions. That's where we make the money.

So I'm going to tell you **EXACTLY** what I do to accomplish both.

But before all that, there's a little $$$ we need to make first.

And that's right after our visitor opts-in. We need a front-end offer.

Why The Front End Offer Is Critical?

You won't make any money unless you get traffic. In order to guarantee that some eyeballs actually see your landing page, you'll need to buy traffic yourself.

Sure, getting organic traffic with the whole "build it and they'll come" approach is a nice fantasy.

And yes, there are some cumbersome ways to get small trickles of free traffic to your squeeze. The reality though, is that if you want traffic – go to the traffic store and buy it!

BUT!!

Buying traffic is pretty darn expensive. And unless we have a larger sized budget, it won't take too long to burn through our advertising spend. The **BETTER** way is to include an offer **IMMEDIATELY** after visitors subscribe.

That way, we can easily pay for traffic and make money at the same time.

If we then reinvest our front-end sales on more traffic, it's not farfetched to have an UNLIMITED supply of visitors to our page.

It Works Like This

Money ==> Traffic ==> Subscribers + Front End Sales (money) ==> Traffic ==> Sales ==> Traffic ==> Sales ==> Traffic ==> Sales ==> Repeat.

… You'll notice that the process just repeats. Every time you buy more traffic, you get two things.

- Sales to reinvest on traffic
- New subscribers

The sales to reinvest on traffic help you in the short term. Without front-end sales, you cannot buy unlimited traffic.

You will eventually run out of money and will have to wait to make money from your subscribers.

The subscribers have a more **LONG TERM** value. These are real people that can/will open your emails for years to come if you do it right.

Building up your list is your primary goal. You do that by investing on traffic. You can only have an unlimited supply of traffic if you make money immediately after opt-in.

What Is A Good Front End Offer?

A good front end offer is a cheap "make money online" product that visitors will buy on impulse.

In general, most people are unwilling to spend anything more than $27. And are A LOT more likely to purchase in the $7-19 range.

Please note that I **do not** recommend only promoting low ticket offers. In fact, your ROI (return on investment) after you've built a relationship, will be much higher with mid-high ticket products.

The low ticket offer is best for the instant after opt-in. Where subscribers are interested in what you're showing them, but not willing to empty their pockets.

Make sense?

We need a cheap affiliate product that will get impulse buys.

Here's one that'll do the trick:

This product is called "$200 in 20 Minutes"

- It costs $9.95 (hits our low-ticket sweet spot)
- Converts at 5% (reasonable amount of visitors buy)
- Includes upsells (chances to make sales after initial purchase)
- Product title geared towards impulse buyers

All-in-all, here's a product that's a good fit for a list building funnel. There are many products just like this one, that can be found at:

- Clickbank
- JvZoo
- Warrior Plus

Each of those sites has hundreds of "make money online" products, with many income possibilities.

Imagine how much money you'll make after you have a list of people that are all interested in making money online. This is powerful stuff!

Setting Up Your Front End Offer

First off, you need an autoresponder service. Aweber is top notch and comes with a 30-day free trial.

Once you have an account at Aweber, you need to set up your web form.

These web forms can be directly installed on your website, but more likely will be integrated into some kind of fancy tool, like WP Profit Builder.

To get to the sign up forms, click on the **"Sign Up Forms"** button on your Aweber navigation bar.

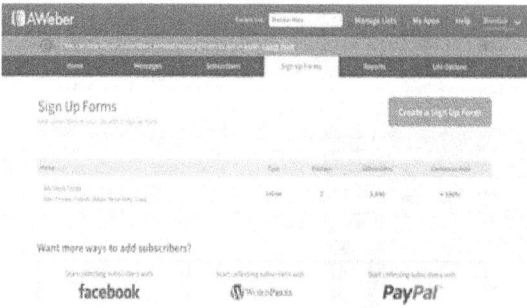

Then, click on the **"Create a Sign Up Form"** button at the top right.

Save your form on the first page…

This next part is where we put our Front End Offer.

We need to grab our affiliate link. We do this by choosing an offer at Clickbank, Jvzoo or Warrior Plus and then we get our link to the chosen product with our affiliate ID attached.

That way, we make money any time someone makes a purchase with our link.

So get that link and enter it on the second page.

Next, **insert your affiliate link**. From Clickbank, Jvzoo, WarriorPlus, etc.

Click on save and move to the final page.

On the last page, click on "**I Will Install My Form**" and then click on the "**Raw HTML Version**"

Now, you can just copy this code and place it onto your squeeze page.

This means that, when someone opt-in on your squeeze page.

You'll:

- Collect the lead
- Redirect them to your affiliate offer

In WP Profit Builder, this is really simple.

The editor has a spot on the right-hand side with the title "Form Code"

Paste the code in there and Profit Builder will take care of the rest.

Looks like this:

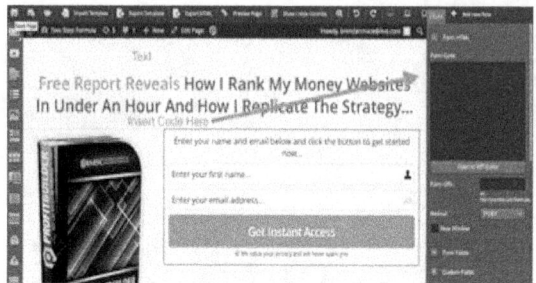

And that's it – the whole process.

Looks complicated, but it's all pretty easy once you get the hang of it!!

Chapter 5 – Easy Way to Get Traffic

Other than cold hard cash, **traffic** is your main asset. You need it. Buy it.

There are many places to buy traffic, but the **EASIEST** way is to buy solo ads.

Here's how it works:

1 You find a solo seller with a solid reputation
2 You buy an agreed upon # of clicks
3 You pay (around .40) for each click

That's it. Easy right?

Where To Find Solo Ads

There are two main places to get solo ads.

1 FaceBook
2 Skype

My preference is FaceBook. Solo sellers on FaceBook have their reputations on the line with every sale. So if you pick someone with an established rep, you're virtually guaranteed to get a decent solo.

Finding FaceBook groups that cater to solo ads is pretty darn easy. Just search for "solo ads" and you'll get a good-sized list of viable solo groups to join.

Here's the one that I own:

https://www.facebook.com/groups/189347897917735/

All of them are 100% free to join.

Find a provider with a good reputation and order your solo.

Here's a few tips, though.

• All solo traffic is pretty much the same, other than tier 1% (getting to that in a second). Don't fall for someone telling you that his traffic is way better. As someone who's purchased over 100 solos, I can say with certainty that traffic quality is comparable. The difference is how related your offer is to the traffic's interests. Ask your vendor what their list is interested in. They should be able to tell you.

• Tier 1% is an important feature. It means how much of the traffic is coming from wealthy countries. Feels weird to discriminate based on global location, but the reality is that US, UK and Canadian traffic is way more likely to actually buy things. Which at the end of the day, is your main goal.

• Prices are almost always negotiable. I've purchased dozens of solo ads and got a discount on the vast majority of them. All you gotta do is ask. Most vendors will drop their prices to close a sale. Solo vendors will be even more likely to offer a discount if you promise to write a testimonial afterwards.

Chapter 6 – Scaling Up + Making Money

Up till now, we've covered squeeze page creation and a traffic strategy that's self-replenishing.

If you keep reinvesting your front-end sales into more traffic, you'll be building your list rapidly.

Getting that big ol' email list is now a reality.

How Much Money Can You Earn With Your List?

The vast majority of the money we make should come on the back end. In marketing terms, the "back end" means all emails and promotions that occur after the initial offer.

I've heard the claim that email lists should make around $1/month per subscriber.

So let's do some quick math.

1 I have 40,000+ subscribers
2 I make about $5,000 a month (from my list)

Okay, so clearly not $1 a month for me. The reality is that there are loads of variables that affect your income per subscriber.

There are marketers with higher earnings per subscriber and marketers with much lower. It's going to depend completely on how you market to them.

The reality though, is that this is about as easy as it gets to make money online. But more on that later.

The Money Is In The Email Sequence

The front end offer enables us to keep reinvesting in more traffic. Which gives us our email list.

The autoresponder sequence is where we make the big bucks.

An autoresponder sequence is a series of emails that are sent to your list after they initially opt-in.

Most autoresponder services, like Aweber, allow you to build it as big and robust as you want. It's a good idea to have a full sequence ready to go.

Here's the first 5 emails in my sequence:

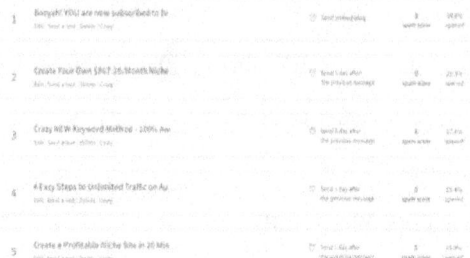

My Aweber sequence currently has 124 follow-up emails. And I still keep adding to it.

The sequence MUST have promotions but it **ALSO** must _add value_ to your subscribers. If you only send promotions, it won't take long for you to burn through your leads.

Burning a list means that subscribers no longer open your emails or click on your links. It's a very bad thing. And it's easily avoidable by adding some value in between your promotions.

My email sequence has a nice balance of value submissions and offers. It's taken me awhile to put together and tweak, but it's been worth it.

Want To Get A Head Start?

Aweber allows marketers to share their email sequences with each other.

It's a badass feature that really does not get used enough in our market.

I'm about to share with you my entire email sequence. All 120+ emails, completely done-for-you.

To get my email sequence, you just need to

    1 Sign up for a 30-day free trial at Aweber
    2 Paste in my "campaign share code"

Campaign Code = awlist4148279-5b487-$F

You just need to copy the sharing code you get above and place it here:

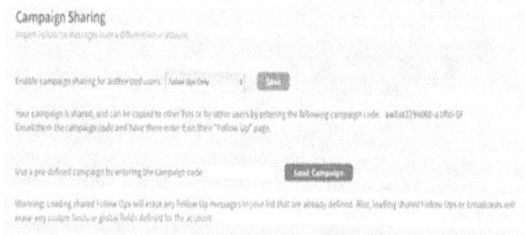

Right where it says "Use a pre-defined campaign by entering the campaign code:"

Paste in the code and it'll upload my entire sequence.

What You Need To Change?

It is not recommended to use these emails "out of the box" so to speak.

There are a few changes to be made-

Change The Branding

These emails use the "Brendan Mace" branding a lot, Especially, at the end the messages. Just go in there and edit the text. Personalize to your name (or company).

Change The Affiliate Links

As it stands right now, the links all have my affiliate ID attached.

This is a really simple fix. All of the products promoted are either from the Clickbank Marketplace or JvZoo. Find out which each product belongs to and get your own affiliate link.

This is crucial. You need your affiliate links in there to make the money.

Add Your Own Stuff

Your funnel is (and should be) different than mine. Add your own stuff in here. Whether that's blog posts, or affiliate promotions. You get to pick where the traffic goes.

Make The Content Unique

If you really want to go the extra mile then you should go through each email and rewrite it so it's unique.

You don't have to write them from scratch, just look at what I have written then tweak it so it says the same thing but in slightly different words.

How Much Can I Make Per Hour?

Here's a list building MYTH that never gets old. I see questions, like *"how much can I make [in 'x' amount of time] from now?"*

This myth makes sense, I mean, people are used to working in 9-5 jobs and expect their income to match the time and effort put in.

It doesn't work like that. For better or for worse.

There are only three metrics that matter!!

1 How much do you EARN per visitor
2 How much are you paying per visitor
3 How much traffic did you buy

Here's a thought provoking question for ya...

If I told you that for every $1 you gave me, I'd give you $2 back.

How many dollars would you give me?

If you were smart, you'd give me near every dollar you have. Because you'd know that for every $1, you'd get $2 back.

The key is to build a funnel that makes more per visitor than you spend on traffic. If you can do that, you've won!!

Here's a time breakdown for you:

- buying traffic takes 10 minutes
- writing an email to send takes 10 minutes

And BOOM... That's it.

20 minutes total.

Once you have a funnel in place, you can literally spend 20 minutes per day on this and easily make a full time income. No joke!!

Living The Laptop Lifestyle

Your most valuable currency is not money – it's time.

Sadly, the 9-5 job-lifestyle swallows it all up. After getting ready for work, commuting to the job and taking care of household chores, most 9-5'ers are left with an hour or less of free time.

What's the point of making money without any *time* to spend it on?

The real advantage of this "20 minute" routine is that it'll give you all the money you need to pay your bills, take that long awaited vacation, provide for your family, even some extra cash to burn on fun.

You can start to live the laptop lifestyle.

Most importantly, though, this business model will give you time.

... What you do with that time is up to you.

But here's some ideas:

- Travel
- Learn a language
- Fall in love

- Stay in love
- Time with your kids
- Improve your funnel

It's not healthy to do all work and no play. You need a balance between the two. And sometimes, you just need to take a break from work altogether and enjoy a well earned vacation

Here's some pictures of my trip to Cuba:

Setting up a passive income business model gives you **FREEDOM!**

Even while you're on a beach in Cuba…

Aweber is still sending mail to your subscribers. That means you're making money 24/7/365. And it only takes about 20 minutes of your time a day to keep it all growing.

Chapter 7 – Bonus Traffic Strategy

So far, I've advised *buying* traffic through solo ads. There is a FREE method, though.

Once you get 800-1000+ subscribers, you can start *trading clicks.*

This works very similarly to buying solo ads. Instead of paying for traffic, you just deliver traffic to a partners page and in turn, get the same amount of clicks back.

It's easy.

How Click Banking Works

1) Go to a clickbanking FaceBook group.

– "Clickbanking" is a fancy word for trading clicks. That's all you need to know.

There's a group here, here and here.

2) Find 5 FaceBook members with several testimonials

– There are TONS to choose from

3) Ask them if they would like to bank clicks with you.

– Make sure to be willing to send first. If you're the newbie on the block and you're contacting established banking partners, its good banking etiquette to send first.

Okay, got some banking partners. Now what?

Your banking partners will give you a *tracking link*. This is how they'll know how many clicks you've sent to their offer.

You also need to create a "trackable link," so that you can send the appropriate amount of clicks to their page.

A free service for link tracking is called Bit.Ly. It's not the best and I'd recommend investing in a better one later. But for just starting out – it'll do the job just fine!!

Then it's easy.

Write up a broadcast email in your Aweber account and include the link to your partner's offer.

Once you've hit the agreed upon # of clicks. Contact your partner and give them a link to YOUR offer.

For Example

You could arrange to bank 100 clicks with 5 partners. Every time you finish sending 100 clicks to a partner, you move on to the next one.

After all is said and done. You'll have sent out around 500 clicks to your partners.

In turn, they'll owe you 500 clicks back. That's **500 FREE visitors** that you don't have to buy.

If you were purchasing a solo ad, that much traffic would cost you about **$200.**

Trading clicks with banking partners is a great way to get FREE traffic.

Conclusion – Wrapping it Up

I've tried to make this blueprint as thorough as possible. I honestly believe that anybody reading through this entry, could easily get a funnel started in the next few days.

If you find videos easier to follow than blog posts, I've created a 3-Part YouTube series right here on this exact blueprint. You'll see everything over my shoulder as I go through the entire process.

I hope you enjoyed reading about my simple two-step formula.

My last piece of advice is this: Don't let *small minds* convince you that your dreams are TOO BIG.

You can do this!!

If you would like to learn more about how to build passive income online, then I would love to chat with you. Check out my blog that shares in depth guides, like this one.

Right here: www.brendanmace.com

www.ingramcontent.com/pod-product-compliance
Lightning Source LLC
Chambersburg PA
CBHW070428190526
45169CB00003B/1454